BLACK AFRICA ON THE MOVE

BLACK AFRICA on the MOVE

by Leslie Alexander Lacy

illustrated with photographs

Franklin Watts, Inc.
575 Lexington Avenue
New York, N.Y. 10022

For Jacqueline Pierce

Photographs courtesy of:
The Brooklyn Museum: page 48 top
Ghana Information Services: page 31
Anthony D. Marshall: page 4
New York Public Library, Schomburg Collection: pages 5, 21
Tanzania Office of Information: frontispiece, page 44
United Nations: pages 13, 14, 16, 17, 18, 19, 22, 24, 26, 28, 30, 33, 34, 36, 37, 39, 42, 48 bottom, 49, 57, 59

Maps by GEORGE BUCTEL

SBN 531–00702–2

Library of Congress Catalog Card Number: 77-75874
Copyright © 1969 by Franklin Watts, Inc.
Printed in the United States of America

4 5

CONTENTS

BLACK AFRICA ON THE MOVE

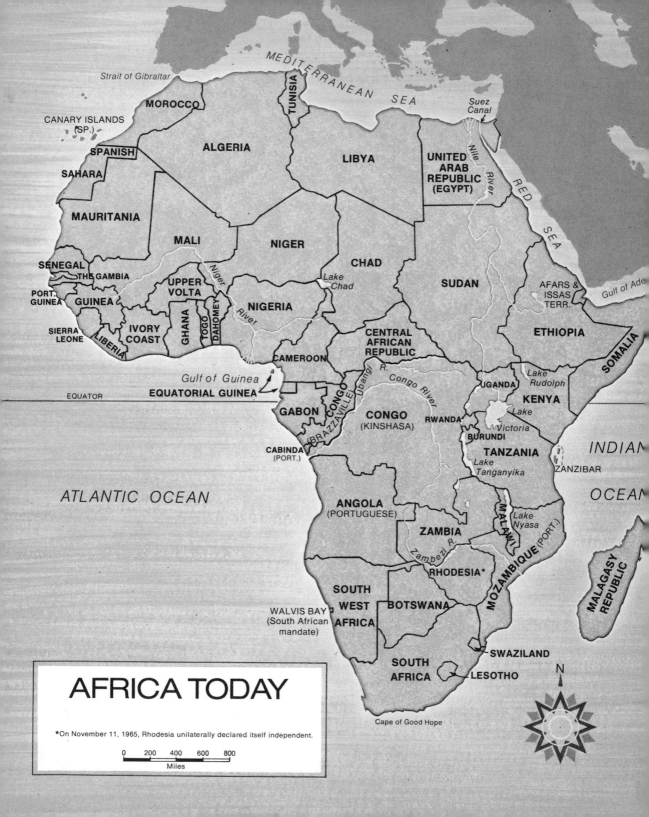

MEDITERRANEAN SEA

Strait of Gibraltar

MOROCCO

CANARY ISLANDS
(SP.)

TUNISIA

Suez Canal

SPANISH

ALGERIA

LIBYA

UNITED
ARAB
REPUBLIC
(EGYPT)

SAHARA

Nile River

RED SEA

MAURITANIA

MALI

NIGER

CHAD

SUDAN

SENEGAL
THE GAMBIA
PORT.
GUINEA
GUINEA

UPPER
VOLTA

Niger

NIGERIA

*Lake
Chad*

AFARS &
ISSAS
TERR.

Gulf of Aden

SIERRA
LEONE
LIBERIA

IVORY
COAST

GHANA
TOGO
DAHOMEY

River

CENTRAL
AFRICAN
REPUBLIC

ETHIOPIA

CAMEROON

SOMALIA

Gulf of Guinea
EQUATORIAL GUINEA

EQUATOR

GABON

CONGO
BRAZZAVILLE

Ubangi R.

Congo River

UGANDA

*Lake
Rudolph*

KENYA

CONGO
(KINSHASA)

RWANDA

*Lake
Victoria*

KENYA
Lake

BURUNDI

TANZANIA

INDIAN

CABINDA
(PORT.)

*Lake
Tanganyika*

ZANZIBAR

OCEAN

ATLANTIC OCEAN

ANGOLA
(PORTUGUESE)

ZAMBIA

MALAWI

*Lake
Nyasa*

MOZAMBIQUE (PORT.)

MALAGASY
REPUBLIC

Zambezi R.

RHODESIA*

WALVIS BAY
(South African
mandate)

SOUTH
WEST
AFRICA

BOTSWANA

SWAZILAND

SOUTH
AFRICA

LESOTHO

Cape of Good Hope

N

AFRICA TODAY

*On November 11, 1965, Rhodesia unilaterally declared itself independent.

0   200   400   600   800
Miles

THE LAND AND PEOPLES OF BLACK AFRICA

Africa south of the Sahara Desert, an area almost three times the size of the continental United States, is known as Black Africa, sometimes called Negro Africa to distinguish it from the Muslim Arab cultures to the north. Some historians have called this division artificial, and today, in fact, many people in both northern and southern Africa do not recognize the distinction.

Again and again one hears and reads of the rich, ancient cultures of northern Africa. Until recently little was said about the lands of Africa south. Now, the world is looking to this part of the continent, seeking to understand its history and its peoples.

Except for seasonal rains and the cooling dry winds from the north, the climate of black Africa is hot and humid. This is the Africa of tropical highlands and treeless plains that stretch across the giant continent from the Atlantic Ocean to the Indian Ocean and where at every turn there are beautiful rivers and lakes. In the west, the original home of most American slaves, are thick

Mount Kilimanjaro in Tanzania (19,321 feet) is the highest peak in Africa.

Wildlife in eastern Africa.

grasses, scattered trees, and poisonous female mosquitoes which carry the deadly disease malaria. In the central part, the Congo region, there is a thick rain forest, where the smaller trees never see the light of day. In the east, around Kenya, Uganda, and Tanzania, are all kinds of wildlife, hills too high for the young Africans to climb, and mountains covered with snow.

Africa south was the cradle of civilization. The remains of what may have been the world's first inhabitants have been found in Tanzania, leading some anthropologists to believe that the forefathers of all the human races lived there. The black race stayed in Mother Africa, but the ancestors of the other races were the men who left and found new homes in Europe and Asia. The early people of Africa were always on the move and that is why it is said that the history of man in Africa is one of constant migration.

The black people who remained produced a rich and glorious culture. They made numerous contributions to the creation of Egyptian civilization, and there is growing evidence that the roots of the ancient Egyptian kingdoms came from Africa south.

The black Africans were hardworking people who reached a high level of civilization. The fourth century A.D. saw the beginnings of the great Kingdom of Ghana. There were other early empires, such as Mali and Songhai. These empires had well-developed systems of government, well-organized commercial centers, and well-disciplined armies, and did much to advance the cause of human knowledge. In their desire for learning and progress, black Africans built the great University of Timbuktu in the West African kingdom of Mali. The university had an

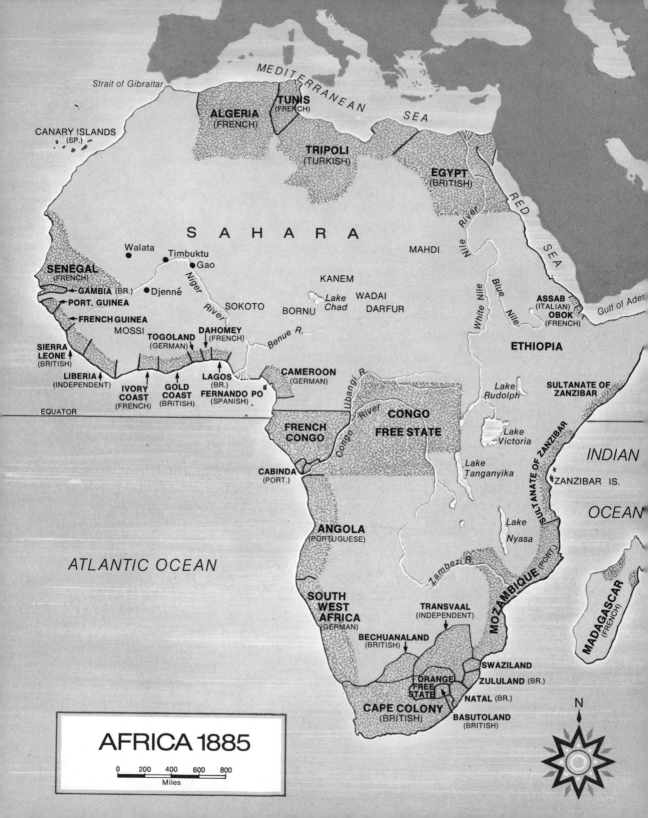

Strait of Gibraltar

MEDITERRANEAN SEA

CANARY ISLANDS
(SP.)

TUNIS
(FRENCH)

ALGERIA
(FRENCH)

TRIPOLI
(TURKISH)

EGYPT
(BRITISH)

S A H A R A

MAHDI

• Walata
• Timbuktu
• Gao

KANEM

SENEGAL
(FRENCH)

Niger River

• Djenné

WADAI

Lake
Chad

DARFUR

RED SEA

→ **GAMBIA** (BR.)
→ **PORT. GUINEA**

SOKOTO

BORNU

Gulf of Aden

ASSAB
(ITALIAN)

→ **FRENCH GUINEA**

MOSSI

Benue R.

OBOK
(FRENCH)

**SIERRA
LEONE**
(BRITISH)

TOGOLAND
(GERMAN)

DAHOMEY
(FRENCH)

White Nile

Blue Nile

ETHIOPIA

LIBERIA
(INDEPENDENT)

**IVORY
COAST**
(FRENCH)

**GOLD
COAST**
(BRITISH)

LAGOS
(BR.)

FERNANDO PO
(SPANISH)

CAMEROON
(GERMAN)

Lake
Rudolph

**SULTANATE OF
ZANZIBAR**

EQUATOR

**FRENCH
CONGO**

Ubangi R.

**CONGO
FREE STATE**

Lake
Victoria

Congo River

INDIAN

CABINDA
(PORT.)

Lake
Tanganyika

SULTANATE OF ZANZIBAR

ZANZIBAR IS.

OCEAN

ANGOLA
(PORTUGUESE)

Lake
Nyasa

ATLANTIC OCEAN

MOZAMBIQUE (PORT.)

Zambezi R.

MADAGASCAR
(FRENCH)

**SOUTH
WEST
AFRICA**
(GERMAN)

TRANSVAAL
(INDEPENDENT)

BECHUANALAND
(BRITISH)

SWAZILAND

ZULULAND (BR.)

**ORANGE
FREE
STATE**

NATAL (BR.)

CAPE COLONY
(BRITISH)

BASUTOLAND
(BRITISH)

N

AFRICA 1885

0   200   400   600   800
Miles

up-to-date library and sent many African scholars to teach in Europe. This was a golden age in Africa.

THE RAPE OF AFRICA

Gradually, over a period of many years, black Africa's golden age came to an end.

Why?

First, military invasions from the Arab north destroyed the empires of Ghana, Mali, and Songhai. With their destruction came the destruction of the University of Timbuktu and the governmental systems. The tribes, which had been united under the great empires, began to fight among themselves.

Second, the slave traders robbed the continent of its manpower. Without manpower it was impossible to build. The strongest and most intelligent young Africans were kidnapped or sold and taken mainly to the Americas where they became slaves.

Before the Africans could recover, along came the third and perhaps most damaging setback. In the middle of the nineteenth century, the military forces of European countries invaded black Africa. They conquered the already weakened African peoples and divided the continent among themselves.

These divisions were artificial and mostly for the convenience of the Europeans. They did not take into account natural geographical features, nor did they recognize tribal units. Many

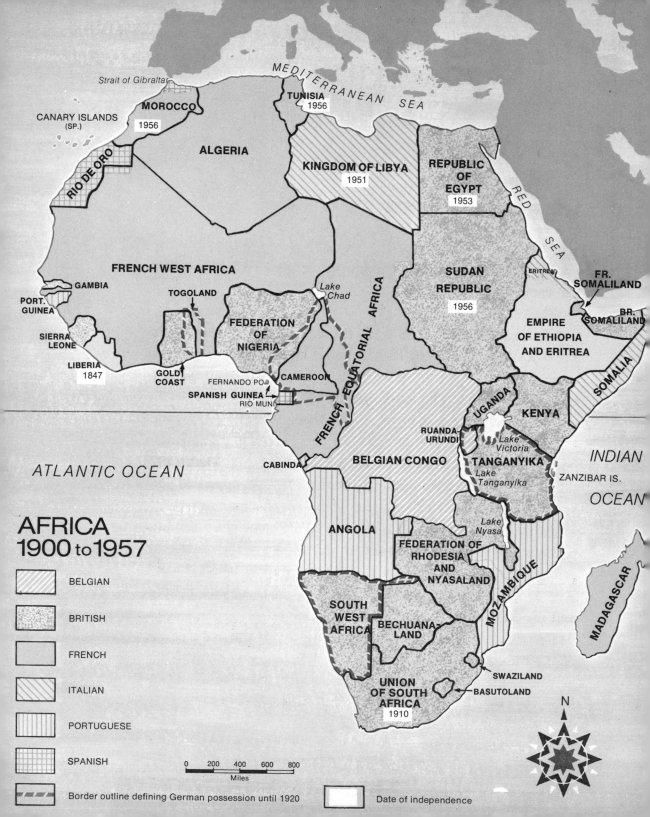

Strait of Gibraltar

MEDITERRANEAN SEA

CANARY ISLANDS
(SP.)

MOROCCO
1956

RIO DE ORO

ALGERIA

TUNISIA
1956

KINGDOM OF LIBYA
1951

REPUBLIC
OF
EGYPT
1953

RED SEA

FRENCH WEST AFRICA

GAMBIA

PORT.
GUINEA

SIERRA
LEONE

LIBERIA
1847

TOGOLAND

GOLD
COAST

FEDERATION
OF
NIGERIA

Lake
Chad

FERNANDO PO
SPANISH GUINEA
RIO MUNI

CAMEROON

FRENCH EQUATORIAL AFRICA

SUDAN
REPUBLIC
1956

ERITREA

EMPIRE
OF ETHIOPIA
AND ERITREA

FR.
SOMALILAND

BR.
SOMALILAND

SOMALIA

CABINDA

BELGIAN CONGO

RUANDA-
URUNDI

UGANDA

Lake
Victoria

TANGANYIKA

Lake
Tanganyika

KENYA

ZANZIBAR IS.

INDIAN

OCEAN

ATLANTIC OCEAN

ANGOLA

FEDERATION OF
RHODESIA
AND
NYASALAND

Lake
Nyasa

MOZAMBIQUE

MADAGASCAR

SOUTH
WEST
AFRICA

BECHUANA-
LAND

SWAZILAND

UNION
OF SOUTH
AFRICA
1910

BASUTOLAND

AFRICA
1900 to 1957

BELGIAN

BRITISH

FRENCH

ITALIAN

PORTUGUESE

SPANISH

Border outline defining German possession until 1920

Date of independence

0 200 400 600 800
Miles

N

tribes, and even families, were separated. For example, one part of the Ewe tribe remained within the boundaries of Ghana, while the other part lived across a border in Togo. Tribes from the Ivory Coast were spread out in Ghana, Liberia, Mali, and Guinea, and tribes in Nigeria had links in Niger, the Cameroons, and Togo. In other parts of Africa the situation was about the same.

At first there was fierce competition among the European powers, but through many compromises they worked out their differences. France, Britain, Portugal, and Belgium took the lion's share. Germany, Spain, and Italy took what was left. In East Africa, where the weather is always pleasant, the English

An African is examined for purchase by white slave traders.

brought their own families from England to settle land that was stolen from African farmers.

With the continent divided and occupied by foreign military troops, the European powers forced upon the Africans a new system of government. Under this system, which is called colonialism, one country takes over another by force for economic gain.

By 1900 there was little left of Africa that was not within the range of a European army post.

The Africans did not stand idly by and watch all of this happen. They did not lie in the sun and say, "Come, Mr. White Man, and rule us." They fought against the invading armies of Europe, but their spears and old-fashioned weapons were no match for the invaders' machine guns and rapid-firing rifles. To make a bad situation worse, Africa made no unified stand. Africans did not stick together. They did not trust each other. During the slave trade some tribes had sold members of other tribes to the Europeans, and as a result the Africans hated and feared and fought one another. Even when faced with a common enemy, which none of the tribes or states could have defeated individually, they failed to stand together.

THE COLONIAL SYSTEMS

Why did Europeans invade Africa and set up colonies? The expansion of Europe into Africa was part of the economic development of Europe. Industries in Europe needed foreign markets and mineral resources. Some European governments needed more prestige and power. Africa offered all these things.

All of the European invaders shared one belief: Europeans were superior to Africans. And believing themselves superior, the Europeans felt it was their moral duty to civilize the African. In fact, the Europeans considered the Africans no more than children. This belief ran throughout the colonial system and served to justify its existence.

Each European power had its own type of colonial rule. British colonialism was very practical. It allowed the Africans to rule themselves so long as African rule did not conflict with British interest.

The French wanted to make Frenchmen of the Africans. They therefore considered Africa a part of France. The French felt that Africans could become civilized by learning the French language and culture.

The Belgians rejected both the British and French styles of colonial rule. Belgians did not even consider the Africans people. They forced the Africans to work in the rich Congo mines and went so far as to chop off the hands of Africans who disobeyed.

The Portuguese plan was similar to that of the French. But neither Portugal, France, nor Belgium allowed Africans even the small amount of political control they had under British rule.

In spite of differences, however, colonial rule in one colony was like colonial rule everywhere else. Its existence meant that the strong and privileged white minority would dominate the weak and underprivileged black majority, distinguishable by the color of its skin. In this respect, all Europeans were the same. However much they may have differed as individuals, all Europeans had a special place in the colonial order.

EDUCATION UNDER COLONIALISM

Education for Africans under the colonial system meant that only a select few were given a primary and secondary education. Usually these were the sons of the small class of wealthy Africans. It was sometimes possible for a boy born to poor parents in a rural area to pass from his village school to secondary school and then to a university in Europe. But this was the rare exception.

The select few attended Christian mission schools. Good students received the equivalent of a high school diploma and went on to England or France for further study. Travel to America was usually discouraged because most colonial educators felt that American universities were inferior to those in Europe.

After World War II, France and England established universities and training colleges in most of their colonies. The students who did not attend college usually found jobs in the civil service. In fact, only a few went on to college. Although pre-college students took basic courses in reading, writing, and arithmetic, these courses did not prepare them for college. The aim of colonial education was to produce clerks and office workers

Students at a boys' Roman Catholic Mission school in Cameroon.

Typing is part of the program offered in commercial schools set up by colonial rulers to produce clerical workers.

for the colonial civil service. The education was designed to develop Africans who could carry out orders efficiently rather than Africans who could think creatively.

All instruction in these schools was conducted in a European language. The use of a European language handicapped the Africans, since the language of instruction was always their second language. In addition, European teachers in most schools discouraged Africans from speaking their tribal languages during school hours.

Africans were taught only European history and culture. African history and culture were not taught because the colonial educators felt that the Africans had not produced a civilization worth discussing.

In the mission schools the Africans were encouraged to despise their familiar gods and traditional beliefs. This separated

A Muslim school in northern Nigeria.

some African mission-school students from the majority of their people. The students who rejected their own culture and were rejected by the Europeans were outsiders in both worlds.

In the Muslim areas the situation was different. The Christian mission schools did not take root. In northern Nigeria, for example, the powerful Hausa people did not adopt western ways. Muslim culture was taught in the Hausa language and was easily accepted. Hausa remained the official language of the local government.

NEW TOWNS OF BLACK AFRICA

In each of the African states, a colonial economy was developed. The European businessmen and traders robbed the continent of its raw materials and precious minerals and set up commercial centers there for the export of cotton, cocoa, coffee, rubber, palm oil, palm kernel, diamonds, and timber. Finished products (consumer goods) were manufactured in Europe, and most of the profits from the sale of these goods stayed there.

The Europeans were the only ones to benefit from new industries. Some farmers in Ghana, Nigeria, the Ivory Coast, and Senegal increased their incomes by selling cocoa and groundnuts to the Europeans, but the great majority of Africans did not benefit from the economic changes in their countries.

As these commercial centers grew, new towns were created

Accra, the capital of Ghana, on the west coast.

to meet the needs of the Europeans. Most of the towns were built near the seaports so that minerals and other resources could be loaded easily onto European ships. Some of these new towns were Dakar, Abidjan, Sekondi-Takoradi, Accra, Lagos, Douala, Brazzaville, and Leopoldville (now Kinshasa) in West Africa, and Kampala and Nairobi in East Africa.

There were towns in black Africa before the coming of the Europeans. The urban communities of Djenné, Walata, Gao, Timbuktu, and Kano existed many centuries before colonization. These were towns in the usual sense of the word; organized with systems of government, independent social and charitable organizations, schools, places of worship, and commercial centers.

But the new towns were much more industrial than the old ones. They were European in character. They looked like small versions of London, Paris, and New York. Africans did not feel as free in them as they had felt in their old towns and in their villages.

Dar es Salaam, capital of Tanzania, on the east coast.

A fishing village in Ghana.

Colonialism and the expansion of the cities demanded manpower. Forced labor and taxes placed on village residents brought many Africans to the towns to work. The village had been the traditional center of African life, but with the migration of Africans into towns, many changes occurred in the villages. These rural areas experienced a slow loosening of social controls on the people, and the old structure of the community began to collapse.

The Africans who came to the new towns formed associations and friendly societies for security and protection. These societies

To keep young people in the rural areas, the government of the Ivory Coast offers many kinds of job training.

New roads make it easier for travelers from rural areas to reach their jobs in larger cities.

and associations, usually based upon tribal origins, helped an African from the village or rural area adjust to the demands of town life. These organizations and friendly societies gave a new-comer food and shelter until he found a job. The newcomer also had a sense of well-being because there was someone around who could speak his language and to whom he could bring and from whom he could receive news from home. Although the groups were organized along tribal lines, members of other tribes were seldom turned away.

When the Africans began to demand independence from Europe, these societies played an important role because they provided the base upon which the struggle for freedom was built.

AFRICA FOR THE AFRICANS

Africans were not alone in their demands for freedom. Friends of the Africans in America and Europe were also trying to help. In 1901, 1917, and 1945, several conferences were called in Europe to raise money and enlist sympathy for the cause of African freedom. Dr. W. E. B. DuBois, an Afro-American, and George Padmore, a black West Indian, were among the organizers of these conferences. Dr. DuBois, the sole organizer of the 1901 conference, was one of the first men in America to raise the demand for a free Africa.

W. E. B. DuBois (1868–1963) was an Afro-American educator and writer who strongly supported the movement for a free Africa.

These friends of Africa, most of whom were of African descent, understood very well the African's problem. They had experienced racial discrimination and injustice in America and Europe. As scholars and educators, they felt that a free Africa was a necessary first step to freedom for black people everywhere. They believed in Africa for the Africans. All of these efforts were worthwhile and did much to support the cause of African freedom. But a totally free Africa was still to come.

BLACK AFRICA BACK ON THE MOVE

World War II gave a forward push to the move for a free black Africa. The war brought about radical changes both outside and

inside the continent. Outside Africa the world was changing. The colonial powers were now weak. France and England were in financial difficulty; Italy and Spain faced internal problems. Germany, who had lost her colonies to England and France after World War I, had been defeated. Freedom, brotherhood, and self-determination for all nations was the cry. Representatives of most of the world's countries met in San Francisco, California, and formed the United Nations. The purpose of this new international body was to prevent wars and bring peace to a troubled world.

The Africans watched these changes. "Would this talk of freedom and brotherhood apply to us? Would our nations finally have the right to govern themselves?" These were the questions Africans asked. The Asian nations of India, Burma, and Ceylon received their independence shortly after the war. The stage for freedom for black Africa was now set.

The world inside Africa had also changed. Colonialism had created a class of militant black men who no longer wanted to be European subjects. Sekou Touré of Guinea summarized their position when he said, "Yes or no, are you for the liberation of Africa?" Discontent could be seen, heard, and felt throughout the continent. African trade unions called for strikes and boycotts of European industries. Students began demanding that African subjects be taught in their schools and colleges. Civil

In 1945, after World War II, many independent nations met in San Francisco to form the United Nations. Seeing these proceedings, Africans, too, wanted independence.

Sekou Touré, president of Guinea, arrives at the United Nations in New York City to address the General Assembly.

servants wanted higher wages, and higher prices were demanded on the European-controlled world market. And finally, African soldiers who had fought well in the armies of France and Britain to defeat Germany were returning home, wanting the same freedom there which they had fought to establish in Europe.

TOWARD INDEPENDENCE

Britain and France acted quickly. They met most of the African demands and promised the African leaders that self-government would come "as soon as the Africans were ready for it."

These concessions satisfied some middle- and upper-class Africans because they had become rich and powerful under European rule and their own security was tied in with that of the Europeans. But most Africans were not satisfied. They wanted complete freedom and independence. They had had enough promises. They wanted immediate positive action.

These Africans also acted quickly. They knew that the only way to gain power was by organizing their people. So in most of the African colonies, nationalist leaders formed political parties. In 1944, the people of the Cameroons and Nigeria formed the National Council of Nigeria and the Cameroons. The Ghanaians organized the Convention Peoples party. The Kenyans organized the Kenyan African National Union, and most of the French colonies united into the African Democratic party.

The leaders who organized these political parties were called nationalists because they wanted to build their own nations. They believed that Africans had always been ready to govern themselves. They wanted their own languages, arts, science, religion, morality, even their own etiquette and fashion. They did not want independence in the near future. They wanted independence *now*.

In order to win rapid independence, the nationalist leaders had to do more than just establish political parties. They had to win over the minds of the people. They had to convince the majority of their fellow Africans that Africans could govern themselves.

Most of the nationalists' attempts to gain freedom were successful and peaceful. However, in some cases the move from European rule to African self-government was not peaceful. In Madagascar, Kenya, the Cameroons, and the Ivory Coast, Africans had to wage violent struggles for their freedom.

In 1957, Ghana, under the leadership of Kwame Nkrumah, became the first colonial territory to gain independence. Guinea followed in 1958. Most of the other African countries received their independence in 1960. In fact, 1960 is called African year.

Africans, such as this young girl, longed for a future in which they would be free.

Kwame Nkrumah, the first president of Ghana.

NEW AFRICA

The government of a new nation, after independence, faces many problems. During the first months of independence, the African leaders in one country after another told their people that independence meant hard work and self-sacrifice.

(28)

The African leaders had to answer many questions:

What kind of government would they have?

What kind of economy would they develop?

What kind of society would they build?

Let us look at the ways in which the different leaders answered these questions:

First, look at the kind of government they would have. Most African nations came to independence by organizing a national party which was strong enough to win political power from the Europeans. After independence this national party formed the new government. These new governments were patterned after the governments of England and France. In the former British colonies the governing body is the legislative assembly, which is divided into the party of government and the party of opposition. This legislative assembly makes the laws for the country in the same way as Parliament does in England or as Congress does in the United States. In the former French states, the legislative body is the general assembly, but it operates like the legislative assembly in the former British areas.

Many Americans and Europeans have criticized the African legislative bodies. They say the African governments are not democratic institutions because most of the men who are elected to these legislative bodies are from the same political party. These foreign critics also say that only a multiparty system can achieve real freedom and equality of representation.

The Africans do not accept these standards. They believe that their forms of government are democratic and best suited to African needs. They feel that the party is open to everyone,

Sir Dauda Jawara, prime minister of the Gambia, delivers an election campaign speech.

even those who might oppose its policies. These same leaders feel that a multiparty system might lead to inefficiency and duplication, which, given the limited skills and resources of their countries, cannot be tolerated. The Africans also remind Americans and Europeans that until democracy has been granted to people of African descent within foreign borders, foreigners have no grounds to speak critically of the forms of African democracy. As former President Nkrumah of Ghana put it: "Americans should practice at home what they preach to us outside."

(30)

Second, what kind of economy would Africans develop? Before an African colony got independence, its economy was still tied to Europe. Independence did not change this very much. Independence gave the Africans political freedom; economic independence was the next step.

Some African nations — Guinea, Mali, Congo (Brazzaville), and Ghana under Nkrumah — believed that the only way to achieve economic independence was through strong governmental direction. They felt that the government should own and control the major businesses, factories, and industries, for only governments can easily and quickly raise the large sums of money that are needed to run the economy.

These leaders felt that it would take too long to build a free

State-owned factories in Ghana.

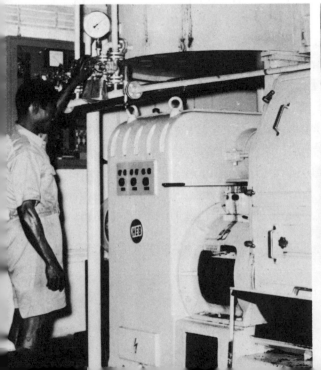

enterprise system like that which exists in America. The desperate hurry of African leaders for economic development is based upon a desire for a high standard of living and a need to fulfill their promises to the poor Africans who put them in office. The leaders also felt that a government-controlled economy would fit in better with the types of governments Africans had before the coming of the white man. Africans do not admire the competitive, dog-eat-dog rules of the Western world. Africans say that they are building a system which is neither eastern nor western but distinctly African.

Other African countries, led by Nigeria, the Ivory Coast, Malawi, and Dahomey, believed that the only way to develop the economy was by allowing and encouraging foreign investment. They felt that Africans did not yet have the knowledge to build all the necessary industries and factories and that free enterprise would best serve their needs.

The African countries with government-controlled economies accuse the free enterprise countries of falling into the enemy's hands. They state that if foreigners invest money in a country, they will not be so interested in helping to develop the country but only in making profits for themselves. And this, they say, is a new form of colonialism.

Third, what kind of society would Africans need? Most African leaders in government and business are trying to build democratic societies in which all people are free regardless of tribe, age, sex, or education. In East Africa, where there are Europeans and East Indians, the leaders are trying to build a multi-racial society.

A large flour mill in the Ivory Coast.

In addition to democracy, Africans also want societies in which there is respect for tradition. They do not want to be told that the old ways and customs are backward. They see nothing wrong with eating with their hands. They do not think themselves primitive because the women carry their children on their backs. Africans are very proud of their traditions and become angry when outsiders make fun of them. One African told me of a European doctor who did not understand the ways or use of some traditional African medicines. The European hurt the

Tradition plays an important part in African culture. Here, one Ghanaian chief attends the installation of another.

feelings of the African traditional doctors because he called the practice of such medicine black magic. The European doctor soon left the country because his African patients all refused to be treated by him. Once the people lost trust in him, the government asked him to leave.

(34)

NEW EDUCATION FOR AFRICA

When the Africans gained control of their own countries, they also took over the operation of their educational systems. The first job was to train African teachers. The second job was to get rid of all the European teachers who thought and behaved as if Africans were inferior. The third, and most important, job was to give the African child an education he could use to help his country. Under the European systems of education, Africans were trained mostly to be clerks. There were also a few teachers, lawyers, and doctors. When Africans received independence they realized that in order to build their countries they needed mathematicians, engineers, contractors, and scientists. Today in modern black Africa, Africans are encouraged to enter these fields.

Africans are taught the value of education and how it can be used to help their countries. In Guinea, the motto in the high schools is: "Not education for education's sake but education for the country."

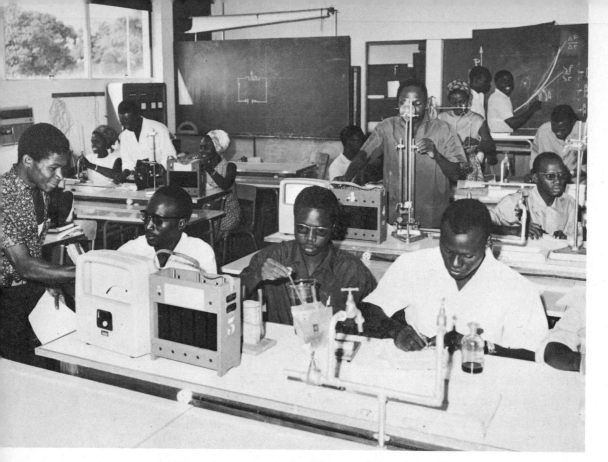

A physics laboratory at a teacher training institute.

The students at the universities are taught not to look down on those who are still unable to read. "If you can read then teach someone else to read," a Nigerian educator has said.

In some African countries, students have to spend their summer vacations working in the fields or in a factory to keep themselves in touch with the way the majority of the people live. These experiences also help students to understand the problems of the working class. One day these same students will hold important positions in government or business and they will have to know what kinds of laws to pass or what kinds of improvements are needed.

African students are very proud. They have a thirst for education. They study hard. In some countries, secondary education is not free and there is fierce competition. Young Africans know that without proper education they cannot develop their countries. Expansion of educational facilities is vitally needed because half the population of Africa is under fifteen years of age and an ever-growing number of students are entering schools.

At the University of Ghana and the University of Ibadan in

Learning land surveying is part of these Asian and African engineering students' training at University College at Nairobi in Kenya.

Nigeria, students stay up very late at night reading and preparing for classes. In Ghana, it is not unusual to see students reading their lessons under the street lights.

Students study hard because they know the future belongs to them. They know that they are leaders of tomorrow. They are taught to believe in their countries. Unlike the former European-run schools, today's African schools teach African history and culture. African students take pride in their heritage and have faith in the future.

A TYPICAL WORKDAY IN AN AFRICAN CITY

Africans get up very early in the morning. Sunrise is about 5:30 A.M. By 9 A.M., Africans have been on their jobs about two hours. They start the day early because they want to get as much work done as possible before it gets too hot.

Every morning there are a lot of trucks in the towns, bringing in fresh food from the countryside. By 10 A.M. all shops are doing business. One sees many individual traders selling their goods on the street. Hundreds of men and women line the sidewalks selling every conceivable type of product. Often the individual traders sell their goods outside one of the big department stores.

These traders are very interesting people. Many of them are

The Sandaga Market in Dakar, Senegal, on the west coast.

very wealthy but sell all kinds of goods just to have something to do. Most of the time there is no fixed price on an item to be sold. The buyer is required to bargain with the seller to get him down to the lowest possible price. Two people can buy identical art objects from the same man and one person might pay three times more than the other. Here the use of an African language and the understanding of African customs are important.

One of the most exciting shopping centers is the marketplace. Hundreds of women (called market women) set up stalls and booths and sell food, clothing, and almost anything one could buy in a variety store. Yet the market shopping center is more than just a place to buy goods. Much of the rich culture of Africa can be found there. Many Africans go there to discuss politics, art, and music. Many of the market women are rich and powerful and exert a strong influence on the government. In all of Africa there are nearly two million market women.

By noon it is very hot. Most of the businesses are closed between noon and 2:30 P.M. This is the hottest time of the day and a lot of people take an afternoon nap. Those who do not sleep sit quietly in restaurants or in the parks playing draughts (the British word for the game of checkers) or reading. The streets are nearly empty, except for a few traders who make it their business to work from sunrise to sunset.

By 3 P.M. the streets are crowded again. Most of the large department stores stay open until 6. The smaller shops and individual traders sometimes sell all night. Those who stay through the night will light a little candle in front of their stalls.

Most Africans spend the early part of the evening with their families. Often groups of families will gather after dinner to talk about politics, listen to folktales, or talk about the good old days in their villages.

By eleven o'clock most people are asleep. Morning comes fast, and another day's work is ahead.

LANGUAGES OF AFRICA

If there is any one feature that shows the great variety of peoples and cultures in Africa, it is language. Out of nearly 2,000 languages in the world, more than 800 languages are spoken in black Africa. Of these, only about 300 have been written down, and most of the writing has been done by missionaries. Within a given territory there may be 20 to 100 tongues spoken. In Ghana, where there are only a little more than 7 million people, there are 55 languages.

In most states the official language is usually English or French. In fact, most people who do not speak an African language are not at a serious disadvantage if they speak English or French. Of course if you do not speak an African tongue, you will probably not learn very much about the people.

It is interesting to watch Africans speak both a European language and a native African tongue. They seem to change in appearance with the change in language. For example, a Ghanaian who speaks both English and Ga (a language of western Ghana) usually speaks English well, but you can tell that he is

A literacy class in French in a Mali village.

not truly at ease and that it is a foreign language for him. But when he speaks Ga, his personality seems to change. Then he is smiling, walking around, and constantly gesturing.

One language (like Akan, a major language in Ghana) may have minor languages which are very similar to it. There may also be several dialects to a language. Some languages are related closely enough that the speakers of one dialect find it beneficial to learn several others.

It surprises many foreigners in Africa (who can sometimes speak only one language) to find so many Africans who speak as many as five languages. Most university students speak six, including good English and French.

Most African children learn a second language before they reach the age of ten. Once in school they must learn the language of instruction, such as English or French. As they grow older they learn more languages. The Africans realize that in order to communicate and develop they must be able to speak to each other.

Although most Europeans do not speak or wish to learn African languages, it is sometimes to their advantage to do so. Missionaries want to convert the people; traders wish to bargain directly; historians and scholars want to translate written records.

African languages are not primitive or backward. African language systems have very complex grammars. After trying to learn Ewe (a language spoken in parts of Ghana, Togo, and Dahomey), a European language such as Spanish or French seems easy.

African languages have characteristics that distinguish them

Youngsters in Tanzania learning to read and write Swahili, their language.

sharply from languages in other parts of the world. Vowels are rare, word stems tend to begin with consonants, and most of the sounds are nasal. The language of the Khoisan people in South Africa makes use of a series of complex clicking sounds. Miriam Makeba, the South African folk singer, has recorded a song known as "Click Song."

Long before the Europeans came, Swahili (the major language of what is now Tanzania) was widely used as the language of trade throughout East Africa. Hausa, the major language of millions of black Muslims in northern Nigeria, has long been the language of trade throughout the western part of Africa.

Today in Africa all governments face the problem of dealing with all these languages. On one hand, the Africans know that the techniques of modern science are written in European languages. Africans must learn the European languages to get the information that will provide them with the skills to develop their countries. On the other hand, many Africans, especially the intellectuals, feel very strongly about their tribal languages. The history and tradition of a people are expressed in its language. Many also feel that if education is conducted in a foreign language African children might suffer an undue handicap.

In the future, most Africans will probably speak as many as six languages, including Arabic and French.

AFRICAN CULTURE

Since the end of colonialism there has been a rebirth of African cultures. The Europeans, including the missionaries, did not feel that the Africans were "human" enough to have created meaningful cultures. Today Africans are showing the world that they not only have a culture but that it is as rich and fine as the cultures of Europe and Asia.

Let us look at the literature first. Literature, like language, expresses a part of the African soul. It has always been that way. Most of the literature is oral. It is usually sung or recited in the form of folktales. In the folktales we see into the heart of Africa; we hear about the legends of tribal conquest, religious ceremonies, battle hymns, drum stories, and lullabies. These tales are rich in emotion.

In the folk songs you feel the day-to-day life of Africa. You listen to songs about planting, loving, giving birth, weaving cloth, pounding yams, building homes, and harvesting. But the folktales and folk songs keep alive the traditions of Africa and are handed down by word of mouth.

To appreciate the oral literature of black Africa, one must understand how the African sees life, the wonder of birth, the mystery of death, and God.

Here is a traditional poem sung by Africans:

> Last remaining, last to go
> A border mark I stand
> Where I a boundary passed . . .
> Some folk unwisely fret
> Under ills they can't stop.
> You who work my loss of kin,
> Know you the will of Fate.

This poem is about the mystery surrounding life and death. Sometimes it is recited at a funeral and sometimes at a birth.

Modern African writers are interested in other problems. Most of them read and write in English or French and have usually lived in white societies.

Most of the modern poems and stories are about the experiences of black Africans living around white folk and the problems of getting along with them.

Listen:

> My simple fathers
> In childlike faith believed all things;
> It cost them much
> And their offspring lost a lot;
> They questioned not the lies of magic
> And fetish seemed to have some logic.

So wrote a Nigerian, Denis Osadebey. He is blaming his fathers and all the fathers of Africa for accepting the lies the white man told them. The sons of these fathers, he says, must find the truth.

One of the most famous poets of Africa is Leopold Sedar Senghor, the first president of the Republic of Senegal. He is very interested in the literature of black people all over the world, and in April, 1966, in Dakar, Senegal, he produced the First World Festival of the Negro Arts.

Africa is also rich in sculpture, dance, and music.

African art ranges from the rock paintings of the earliest Africans to the world-famous bronze sculptures of the ancient kingdom of Benin in Nigeria and to contemporary wood carvings, paintings, and gold work. African sculpture is highly advanced.

This wooden fertility doll of the Ashanti people in Ghana is an example of African artistry in wood carving.

An African craftsman carves a drum.

Like the oral literature, the sculpture (statues and masks) tells a story. It shows us how people feel in their society and what they feel about the universe.

European painters, including Paul Cézanne and Pablo Picasso, have been greatly influenced by African artists, especially by their sculpture and masks.

African dance and music, like African sculpture, are highly expressive. They too tell a story. Dance and music play as large a part in African culture as television and baseball do in American culture — they are a basic part of life. There is a dance for every aspect of life.

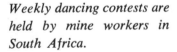

Weekly dancing contests are held by mine workers in South Africa.

What distinguishes the African's dance and music is the rhythm and the use of drums. Since the major function of African music is to communicate, drums are very important. They send messages from village to village, and during colonialism they were used in the struggles against the Europeans. Today most African children learn to play the drums.

SOUTH AFRICA: A TROUBLE SPOT

South Africa is one of the trouble spots in black Africa. The trouble started about four hundred years ago when Europeans landed on the coast. The Zulu tribe that lived on the coast did not want the Europeans to settle there.

The Zulus fought the Europeans, but like other tribes in black Africa they did not have the military strength needed to defeat the Europeans and they lost. The white settlers have been there ever since.

Today in South Africa, there are two nations. The first is a nation of fewer than 4 million whites. This minority controls the economy and the armed forces and keeps the second nation of 13 million black people poor, uneducated, and in slavery. South African black men call themselves Africans, and the white colonists call themselves Afrikaners.

The black nation in South Africa considers the white men in-

To obtain work many Africans in South Africa must leave their village homes and move to overcrowded cities.

vaders. The blacks want their land back and they want the whites to get out.

The white invaders from Europe do not accept these arguments. They say that when they settled the land along the coast, it was uninhabited. Like the European colonialists in other parts of black Africa, these white settlers consider the African people inferior. The strange thing about the whole situation is that the colonialists consider themselves to be very religious people. In

Black Africans work long, hard hours in South African mines.

fact, they quote the Bible to prove that black people are inferior. By making the blacks seem inferior, and therefore less than human, the whites do not have to apologize to the world for the inhuman treatment they inflict on black Africans.

Black South Africans are forced to live and work in conditions that would be unfit for pigs. They are forced to carry name tags and identification cards. They have no civil rights. If they protest they are put in jail and if they try to change the inhuman conditions under which they live, they are killed. They are in effect treated like foreigners and criminals in their own country, the country that was taken from them four hundred years ago. The only crime of which they are guilty is being black.

Many black Africans have died in South Africa fighting for their freedom. One of the greatest Freedom Fighters to die at the hands of this white injustice was Nelson Mandela, who was executed by hanging. He is one of the heroes of black Africa.

It is hard to struggle for freedom in South Africa. Many Africans have had to leave the country. You will find them all over the world raising money and support for their cause.

Black Africans place much of the blame for South Africa's tragedy on the Americans. The blacks point out that many American businessmen and bankers continue to do business with South Africa. Economic strength benefits the present government and enables the country to preserve its racist policies.

One South African Freedom Fighter told me in England, "Americans are hypocrites. They talk about freedom for the South Vietnamese but no American President has yet recommended sending the Marines to South Africa to help the black Africans achieve their freedom."

Most governments in the world have criticized South Africa and she is constantly condemned in the United Nations by African nations, but more than talk is necessary. The black South Africans want action that will help destroy South Africa's existing government and its injustices.

BLACK FREEDOM FIGHTERS

While thirty-seven black African states are free and on the move to economic and political development, Angola, Mozambique, South-West Africa, South Africa, and others are still fighting Europeans for their freedom. The men who are fighting for independence in these countries are called Freedom Fighters. They are young, strong, and courageous men. They are black and beautiful men.

Yet they are lonely men. For long periods of time they are away from their homes. They leave their wives and children behind. Their worldly possessions are few. They own a pair of old boots, a uniform, a canteen for water, and a gun.

These young men were not always violent. At first they were men of peace. They believed that through peaceful demonstrations and pressures from the outside world, their European masters would give them freedom. But these men of peace were mistaken. They found that the Portuguese in Mozambique, Guinea and Angola; the British in Southern Rhodesia; and white South Africans in South-West Africa and South Africa had no intention of giving them freedom.

So each peaceful demonstration was met with more violence. Seeing that black Africans could not get their rightful independence by peaceful means, the men of peace became violent. Today these Freedom Fighters are conducting an armed struggle for freedom in southeastern and southwestern Africa.

But not all Freedom Fighters are soldiers. Some are intellectuals, some are students, some are scientists. They are in many fields. These men are not gunfighters because they know that a revolution to take over a society must produce more than just soldiers. It must also produce men who can govern a society once it is free. A society must have doctors, ministers, social workers, scientists, and plumbers.

So while some men do the shooting, other men are studying and preparing in the capitals of the world so that they will have something to give their people once independence has been achieved. These nonfighting Freedom Fighters also raise money for guns and food in New York, London and Paris for those who are fighting back home.

The struggle is hard, the battles are many, but they know that justice is on their side. They know that they will win. They believe as the great African Freedom Fighter David Diop believed:

> Africa my Africa
> Africa of proud warriors . . .
> Despite the wounds of his broken body
> Keep the bright color of a
> bouquet of hope. . . .

AFRICA AND THE WORLD

Africa has had a great impact on the modern world. Most African countries have moved in less than ten years of independence toward political freedom and economic advancement.

African nations have entered the international community. They all have representation in the United Nations, even though many African countries feel that the U.N. does not always represent their best interests. African nations have representatives all over the world, and they have as many diplomats and civil servants in their foreign services as do some of the major European powers.

The world's big powers are watching Africa's development. Through the Peace Corps and various forms of aid programs, the United States is trying to win Africa over to her point of view. The Soviet Union — America's competitor — is trying through various trade missions to convert Africans to her brand of politics.

Most Africans do not want to move East or West. Yet this

President Dioro Hamani of Niger prepares to address the United Nations General Assembly in 1967.

position is difficult to maintain. Africans depend upon both the East and West for foreign aid. Few people, however, really know which way Africa is moving. Every day something changes.

Africa still has many problems. One of the most serious problems is tribalism. Tribalism is the strong loyalty felt by many Africans to their ethnic group, or tribe. Before colonialism and after the breakup of the great empires, African life revolved around the tribe. The center of the tribe was the family, which was usually very large and spread out. In the new African towns, there are people of many different tribes. The members of these groups often compete for jobs, and the tribes enter into rivalry with one another. Ethnic hostilities grow and tribalism becomes more pronounced than it was in the villages, where there seldom was close contact between tribes. If African leaders want to build strong nations, they must make tribalism work for and not against their goal. Even today, some Africans are more loyal to their tribe than they are to their nation. Nigeria is a good example of the inability of tribalism to work in harmony with the modern structure of government. The Ibo tribe, unable to work out its difficulties with the federal government, broke away from Nigeria and formed the new state of Biafra. The Nigerian government opposed this move. And the result was a civil war between the Nigerians and the Biafrans.

Another problem throughout Africa is corruption in office. In many countries where public officials are paid low salaries, it has become common practice for such officials to accept bribes in exchange for various favors. Some officials hold positions in which they can easily pocket government funds. This is especially unfortunate in Africa, where most nations already have limited resources. In some cases the army has taken over the government in an attempt to stop corruption. Most observers, however, feel that corruption is on the decline.

In spite of these problems, most African leaders are optimistic about the future. They are cooperating more among themselves. In 1965, they formed the Organization of African Unity. The

Young Africans will help to build a better world.

African nations represented in this body feel that it will serve to unite and develop the continent.

But the problems of African nations, like the problems of other countries, cannot be solved in one generation. Africa must be ready for the hard road ahead. To quote the Afro-American writer Richard Wright: "What will happen in Africa will spread itself out over the decades of time and a continent of space . . . There will be much marching to and fro."

Black Africa is on the move once again, and this time it will not be stopped.

INDEX

ABOUT THE AUTHOR

LESLIE ALEXANDER LACY, aged 31, was born in Franklin, Louisiana. He is presently a lecturer on political and social change in the African studies program at Howard University.

Mr. Lacy holds a B.A. and M.A. in political science from the University of Southern California, and an M.S. from the Institute of African Studies at the University of Ghana for his work on trade unions and political change in Ghana.

During his three-year stay in Ghana, Mr. Lacy was an instructor in the department of politics at the University of Ghana. In addition to his extensive travels in Africa, he has traveled to Europe and the Soviet Union.

He has published the following works: "Trade Unions and Government" in *Politics in Africa — 7 Cases,* co-authored with St. Clair Drake and edited by Gwendolyn Carter, (1966); "African Responses to Brother Malcolm" in *Black Fire,* edited by LeRoi Jones and Larry Neal, 1968. He is currently at work on a political autobiography.